PUPPY SLEEP TRAINING

THE COMPLETE STEP BY STEP GUIDE FOR A HAPPY PUPPY OWNER!

JACK REES

KOLMEBOOK

CONTENTS

INTRODUCTION

Bringing home a new puppy can be a great experience for the whole family. You and your kids will be able to enjoy the new addition, teach them new tricks, play with them, and give them endless love. Many families dream about getting a new puppy for a long time before they take the plunge and they think that the whole situation is going to be perfect.

While bringing that puppy home is a great idea, many people start to regret it after a few nights of barely getting to sleep. Between hearing the puppy whine to having to get up and take them to the bathroom a ton of times, you are probably feeling exhausted and hopeless.

The good news is that this guidebook has the tips and strategies that you need to turn it all around. We are going to take some time to look at all the preparation that you need to do, as well as the three main strategies that work the best for most families to help them finally get their puppies to sleep. From the light sleeper method to the alarm clock method, and the heavy sleeper method, you are sure to find a sleep training strategy for your puppy that will work like a charm and will help you, your family, and the puppy finally get some much needed sleep at night time.

When you have brought up a new puppy and are ready to finally get some sleep and feel more refreshed and happy about having a puppy in your home, make sure to check out this guidebook to learn all the steps that you need to get started with sleep training your puppy today!

THE BENEFITS OF SLEEP TRAINING YOUR PUPPY

Sleep training your puppy is so important to everyone in the whole family. It helps to stop the whining from your puppy and can allow you, your family, and even the puppy to get on a good schedule together that also includes plenty of sleep.

There are a ton of benefits to everyone in the family, including the puppy, for getting the puppy on a good sleep schedule. Some of these benefits of sleep training your puppy include:

- **Helps you to get more sleep:** If you have spent a few nights listening to the puppy and having to take them outside a million times each night, then you are probably feeling pretty exhausted at this point. While sleep training methods still take a few more days before you see them completed, they are the right steps that you need to take to finally get your nights back for some good sleeping.
- **Can avoid accidents at night:** If your puppy is up and moving and active in the middle of the night most nights, it is not going to be long before they have an accident. The more that the puppy is up, the more likely that they will have this accident. With a good sleep training procedure, you not only help teach your puppy how to sleep through the night, you also help to train them to go outside at certain times so you will deal with fewer accidents.
- **Let's the family sleep:** Not only do you

need to get some sleep, but so does the rest of your family. If everyone is up in the middle of the night because the puppy is barking and making too much noise, it can be hard on everyone. Even if you are the only one getting up in the middle of the night to take care of the puppy, it does not mean that others are not hearing the puppy whine and bark and moving around. And it will not take long before this starts to wear on everyone nerves. Helping the puppy learn how to sleep train can really make a difference in the quality of sleep that everyone in the family is able to get.

- **Helps your puppy get their days and nights in order**: Just like it is important for you and others in your family to get enough sleep at night so that you are all energized and ready to tackle the day, so does your puppy. If they get things mixed up, they are going to miss out on a lot of fun during the day playing with other people, going on walks, and more. Helping them learn to sleep through the night with sleep training can get them on a good schedule and makes life easier on them, as well as on you.

- **Allows the puppy to be comfortable in their new home**: When the puppy has some order and knows how things should be done and where they should do them, they are more likely to feel comfortable with that. And sleep training will make this process easier.

- **Allows for different times for play and for sleep:** You need to make sure that your puppy knows that there are times for sleeping, times for eating, times for playing, and so on. Some puppies sleep so much during the day that they get things confused and will have almost limitless energy in the middle of the night. Unless you want to be up with them all night and then head in to work, it is best to start working on a sleep training program with them right away. When the puppy learns to sleep properly at night, they are more likely to learn that day time is the best time to play.

WHEN IT COMES to sleep training, there are so many things to keep in mind. But remembering the benefits, and how much extra sleep you will be able to get when it is all done, will make the whole process worth it.

HAVING A GOOD DAY CAN SET YOU UP
FOR A GOOD NIGHT

T o make sure that you are able to get your puppy to fall asleep and sleep well during the night, there are certain steps that you can take during the day. If your puppy spends all day sleeping, and they do not get enough chances to go outside and go potty, or even if they eat or drink when it is close to their bedtime, then you are in for a long night. With some good planning and some positive actions during the first few days with your puppy, it will not take long before your puppy is falling asleep, and staying asleep, through the night.

So, the first thing that you need to do is make sure that the puppy is active and busy during the day. If they are an older puppy, or an adult dog that is transitioning into your home, make sure to take them on long walks, as long as they don't seem overwhelmed or stressed by the surroundings. With a new puppy on the other hand, you may not be able to take them out on walks yet because they are not properly trained to walk with a leash and they may not have their vaccinations to keep them healthy.

If this is the case with your puppy, then you will need to find ways to keep the puppy moving. You can play with the puppy, have some people over to meet the puppy, and give them lots of chew bones and toys to play with. If you are not at home and can't keep the puppy active during the day all the time, then see if there are some friends or neighbors who can do this for you. A dog walker or a pet sitter can be nice as well to make sure your puppy is as active as possible during the day.

Now, some puppies are really energetic and love to bounce around and play all day. Others may be a little more mellow and may need some convincing to stay active rather than falling asleep during the day. Sometimes it is as simple as changing the environment that is around the puppy. If they like to get cozy in the house and sleep, then take them out back so that they can see the new sounds, smells, and sights.

Of course, it is important to remember that your puppy does need a lot of sleep so some small naps are perfectly normal. As long as they are not napping all day and they get up and move around enough, then it is fine for them to have those naps. However, about three to four hours before you want to go to bed, do not let the puppy sleep. If you let the puppy sleep too much right before bedtime, they will have a hard time sleeping when you want them to.

ANOTHER THING that you should remember here is that what goes in needs to come out. If you are good about setting up a water and food schedule for the puppy during the day, it can help prevent surprises in the middle of the night. Most puppies are going to eat somewhere between three and four meals a day. You must make sure that this last meal is at least a few hours before they go to bed. This allows the puppy to have some time to empty themselves before it is time to go to bed. Three hours before bedtime is best, but try to not let it get any closer than an hour or two. If you are concerned about this eating schedule, it is best to talk with your vet to see what they recommend.

YOU WILL FIND that the whole process of feeding the puppy is going to need some trial and error. Not all puppies are going to respond to the same type of feeding schedule. If you find that your puppy needs to eat right before bed, or closer to bedtime than the three hours, try to make that meal smaller. This can help them to make it through the night.

IF YOU HAVE a puppy who wakes up in the middle of the night fussing because they are hungry, then pushing the eating time back to three hours before bedtime may not be the best. You can also try giving them some small snacks, like a dog biscuit, right before they fall asleep. This is a good way to settle their tummy and even a little water is known to help too. Just make sure that they are not eating or drinking a whole bowl right before bed, or you are going to be up during the night many times.

IN ADDITION, the area where you will put the puppy down to go to sleep needs to be calm and relaxing. It should not have all their toys around it and you should not spend the daytime hours making it fun to use. If you put in toys to the sleep area, you will find that the puppy wants to be playful and active. And if you play in the bedroom often, how is the puppy supposed to learn the difference between playtime and bedtime. There should be separate areas for play time and sleep time. It is fine to hang out or cuddle with the puppy in the sleep area during the day, but no games, such as tug of war or wrestling with toys in that area or you will have one confused puppy.

ONE PROJECT that you should concentrate on during those first few weeks with the puppy during the day is to teach them the command you want to use when it is time to go potty. This will be useful because it helps you to get the puppy outside and using the bathroom before bedtime. This will take a few weeks for the puppy to learn how to associate the word with the action, so be patient and keep trying. Then, once they have been trained with that word, make sure to use it before bedtime to help the puppy relieve themselves.

AND OF COURSE, you need to spend some time acclimating your puppy to their pen or crate if this is where you want the puppy to sleep at night. They need to be comfortable with the crate or the pen, otherwise they are going to get nervous and will not easily fall asleep. With a new puppy, all these experiences are new to them so take it slowly, follow the lead for your puppy, and show them what you expect out of them. But making sure that they have a comfortable place to fall asleep at night will make a big difference in whether they fall asleep and stay asleep, or if they are whining and causing you to be up most of the night instead.

IF YOU DO NOT HAVE a good day with the puppy, it is going to be really hard to get them to fall asleep for you when night time comes around. Think of it this way, if you spend all day sleeping, how likely is it that you will spend the night sleeping as well? Just because you were busy and active at work all day does not mean that your puppy got all that activity while they were home alone. It is your responsibility to make sure that they are worn out at night so they are more likely to sleep.

THERE ARE a lot of different ways that you are able to do this, and we did spend some time talking about them already. You are able to take them on a walk when you first get home. This is good for both of you to do. If you have a puppy, make sure to leash train them first so they are more comfortable on the walk and only go the distance that they are comfortable with. If this is pretty short, you could do a small walk when you first get home and then a longer one before bed to really wear them out. As they get older, you can make the walk longer and really get in some exercise.

PLAY TIME IS important as well. If you have children,

include them in on this to have some fun. Have a variety of toys for the puppy to play with, both inside and outside, and just have some fun. You can play fetch, tug of war, or anything that gets the puppy up and moving. Just make sure that you simmer it down and relax a bit from the really rambunctious games right before bed or the puppy will be too hyper to calm down and go to sleep.

TRAINING the puppy can be a good idea during this time as well. This not only helps to get rid of some of the pent up energy that they have, but it can also help them to work out their minds, which can make them sleepy as well. Start out with some of the most simple commands, such as stay, sit, rollover, shake, and then build up or practice those as you are ready. Include everyone in the family so that they can teach the puppy some new tricks and the puppy learns that everyone can be in charge in the home.

OF COURSE, always remember to not feed the puppy too much and too close to bed. You do not want the puppy to be hungry, but if they load up too much on food and snacks right before bed, it is only going to be a few hours before they are ready to get up and be let outside again. Allow enough time before bed for the puppy to eat and then for them to go to the bathroom a few hours later to relieve themselves so they will sleep better.

———

AND FINALLY, take some time to make their room or sleeping area as comfortable as possible. With a puppy you just brought home, you may want to let them sleep with you and then move them to another area or to their crate later on. You can make that decision, just make sure that the puppy is going to be comfortable in their sleeping arrangements before it is time to go to bed.

———

THIS MAY SEEM like a lot of work in the beginning, but it is necessary to ensure that your puppy feels good and will get some good sleep at night. The more active you can keep them, the more comfortable their bed, and the less they need to go to the bathroom before bed, the better you will be able to sleep that night.

3

WHERE SHOULD I PUT MY PUPPY TO SLEEP?

The next question to consider is where you would like to put the puppy to sleep. This location is going to depend on you and your family. Some families like to have the puppy right next to them so they can spend more time together. Others are not that fond of the idea of having a shedding or snoring beast in their bedrooms, so they will pick another location. There are many options that you are able to choose from when it comes to the sleeping location for your puppy, and you need to pick the one that you think works the best.

FIRST, you must decide where the puppy needs to sleep, right from the start. This may or may not be the same area you want to use when you pick a spot for them permanently because sometimes it is best to keep the puppy near you when they first come home. Most dogs are considered pack animals and they feel more comfortable when they are able to be near other people.

THIS IS true whether you are dealing with a puppy or a grown dog. Some people choose to keep the puppy in the same room as them well into adulthood just because it feels more comfortable to the dog and can make sleeping at night easier on everyone in the home.

You can always move the puppy to another place in the home once they are older and a bit more comfortable. Even if you do not plan to make this a permanent thing, having the puppy spend the first few nights with them can help them feel more secure and comfortable in this new environment and can actually help them make it through the night faster.

If you do decide to have the puppy sleep in one place and then you want to change that location later when the puppy gets older, that is fine. But you must remember that this is going to add in some more steps to the process. You may find that you have to retrain the puppy again to get them used to a new sleeping location.

Some puppies do this well and it only takes a few nights or so to get them to switch over. Others may need to go through the process all over again to get comfortable with a new sleeping location. It is fine to go through this to get them in the right spot, it is just something that you need to keep in mind when choosing a place.

AFTER YOU HAVE HAD some time to train the puppy and show them how to sleep through the night, then you can make a personal decision about where they should sleep on a more permanent basis. You could choose to let the puppy continue sleeping with you as this is considered beneficial to them, but if another room in the home works better, this is fine as well. You can choose a place such as the laundry room, kitchen, or another chosen room. Some owners choose to let their dogs have free reign to sleep where they want at night, but you must make sure that you have broken them of destructive habits.

NO MATTER where you choose to have the puppy sleep, when they are young and first getting started, you must confine them in some way. Otherwise, you are going to find a mess, including chewed-up shoes, all over the home. Some of the places you can choose that will ensure that your puppy stays safe, comfy, and won't get into trouble include:

- **Inside their crate:** if you are already working to crate train your puppy, it is just fine if you choose to have them sleep in this crate. Just make sure that this place is comfortable for them. Add in a few soft toys for company, some good bedding, and that the puppy has had some exposure to this crate before you try to make them sleep in there. You can also consider turning the crate in a way so that the puppy is able to see you while they are sleeping.

- **In a pen**: A wire exercise pen can be a good place to put the puppy to sleep if you are using potty pads to teach them how to use the bathroom. You can pick out a pen for them to sleep in at night, as long as it is just large enough to fit the potty pads and the blanket for them to sleep on. This will help the puppy to figure out the sleeping and potty arrangements faster. If you use a pen, make sure to set it up in the area you want to use permanently to make the puppy more comfortable.

- **Dog bed**: If you would like to start having your puppy sleep in a dog bed, you do not want to just set it down and hope that it will all work out. You want to make sure that the bed is somewhat confined so that they are not able to wonder off and make a mess. One good idea is to set up the dog bed between the wall and your bed. This allows for a small area where you can place the bed, and then you just have a little space to block off with a gate or some kind of barrier.

- **In your bed**: Some people choose to have the puppy sleep in their bed, either temporarily as they get used to the new environment or permanently. You need to make sure that you are able to keep the puppy on the bed so they do not wander off while you are sleeping and cause a mess and so that they do not fall off the bed and get hurt. Most of the time it is best for you to just save this until the dog is older and can handle staying asleep on the bed.

As you can see, there are a number of different options that you can use when it comes to training your puppy and where you would like them to sleep. Sometimes the method that you use in the beginning when you first bring the puppy home will be different than the options that you resort to later on when the puppy is trained and a little bigger. You can choose the method that seems to work the best for you and your family and for the puppy so that you can finally get some sleep at night.

4

PREPARING YOUR PUPPY FOR BED

N ow that you have spent some time learning about how to get your puppy prepared to go to bed at night and you have even thought of some places where you would like the puppy to sleep, it is time to prepare your puppy for bed for the best results.

As it gets close to bedtime, a little planning and preparation will make sure that you and your puppy will be able to get a good night's sleep. It is not going to work to just jump into bed and then hope that the puppy will fall asleep just like you. You do need to put in a little bit of work to see it become a reality.

First, there is something important that you need to consider before you get started with any of this. It is important for you to set a bedtime that is reasonable for your puppy. You must also have reasonable expectations for how long the puppy will be able to sleep at night. So, just because you put the puppy down for bed at eight does not mean that they are going to be completely asleep for the rest of the night. If they go to sleep at this time, then they will probably be up at two in the morning ready to play.

Many people have trouble with keeping their puppies asleep during the night and don't understand that perhaps they are letting the puppy go to bed too early. If you go to bed at eleven at night, but expect the puppy to go to sleep at eight and still sleep until you get up, that is too long. Most puppies are not going to make it past six or seven hours, maybe eight as they get older, before they need to go to the bathroom. It is usually best to schedule the puppy to go to bed when you go to sleep to make life easier.

———

WHILE YOU ARE GETTING ready for bed, set out some of the things that you may need in the middle of the night. It is likely that when you have a new puppy, you will need to get up a few times to let them out. Rather than fumbling around in the dark when they are ready to go out, make sure that everything is set and that you have a nice clear path to walk through at night.

———

THERE ARE a number of things that you can prepare for this. For example, unless your back yard is covered completely and you live in an area that gets really nice temperatures, you should make sure that you have a robe or something else to wear while you are in the backyard. You can also keep your shoes, your glasses, some treats, and other things right there in case you need it. If you are going somewhere that does not have the best light, consider having a flashlight ready so that you are able to see what the puppy is doing and make sure that they will not get lost while going potty.

WHILE YOU ARE AT IT, make sure that the path that goes from your bed to wherever the puppy is located is as clear as possible. Tripping can be a hazard when you get up with the puppy in the middle of the night. You can even consider having a nightlight around to make it easier to see what is going on around you when you get up in the middle of the night.

ANOTHER THING that you can consider is having either a white noise machine or a loud fan that is ready to go wherever the puppy is going to be sleeping. This is a big help because the steady noise is really soothing for most puppies and is really good at masking some of the noise that are outside and may wake up the puppy. If you choose to use a fan for this though, make sure that it is pointed away from the puppy so they do not get cold.

YOU CAN ALSO CONSIDER USING a towel or a blanket. If you notice that the puppy seems a little fussy in their crate and they do not need to be let out to go potty, they may do better if you take the time to cover their crate. For some puppies, this is calming. Just make sure that you check the crate to see if there is enough air flow and that the temperatures do not get too hot inside the crate.

SOME PEOPLE HAVE ALSO TRIED another trick. For this, they will take a ricking close and a hot water bottle, wrap them in a towel, and put them in with the puppy to help make it easier to sleep at night. The point of doing this, according to some dog owners, is to help the puppy remember the heartbeat and warmth of their mommy so that they can get comfortable and go to sleep. The puppy will be reminded of their mother and the warmth and comfort that they felt when they were with her and for some puppies, this is the easiest way to get them to fall asleep.

STUDIES ARE STILL OUT on whether this one will work but if you like the idea, it certainly is not going to hurt anything to give it a try. You can even try using a plush puppy sleep toy that has a warmer or a heartbeat inside so that your puppy can enjoy a little bit of company while they are sleeping at night.

***

AND OF COURSE, the final thing that you must do before you put the puppy down, after their beds are as comfortable as possible, is take them out one more time to go to the potty. Do this about ten to fifteen minutes before bed, and then again right before bed, so that the puppy has plenty of time to go and can get all those distractions out of the way. This helps to empty out the puppy and can save you a lot of hassle, and possible accidents, when you wake up in the morning. If you are dealing with a young puppy, it is likely that you will still need to get up a few times at night to take them out, but it won't be long before you can stop doing this as well.

***

SETTING things up so that the puppy is able to easily go to sleep can make such a difference for how much sleep you get. Make sure that the puppy does not nap too much, that they stay up long enough at night, and that they have an empty bladder and are as comfortable as possible. If you are able to maintain those steps and the other steps in this chapter, you will find that it is much easier to get your puppy to go to sleep, and stay asleep longer, at night.

5

COMING UP WITH A PLAN

A t this point, it is time to make your own plan for surviving the night with a new puppy. There are actually three methods that you are able to use, but before we get into a discussion about each one, here are a few basics that will apply to all the methods of overnight training, no matter which path you decide is the best for you.

FIRST, you need to consider the situation and what your puppy is going through. It is likely that you got the puppy right from their mother and they are used to having that warmth, as well as the warmth of their littermates, around them. Even if you had a stray who you got from the pound or a shelter, you are still bringing them in to a new environment that they may be a bit cautious about.

WHAT THIS MEANS is that the first step that you should take for sleep training is going to include spending time soothing and comforting the new puppy so that they are able to relax before learning that night is when they should sleep. You most likely will need to let them sleep next to you for company, even if you want to have them sleep in their own room later on.

ONE WORRY here is that you will spoil the puppy and never be able to train them to sleep on their own. The truth is, the puppy will actually have a better time sleeping on their own later on if they got to spend the beginning time with you compared to those who were left alone right from the beginning. Even if you only spend a few nights sleeping with the puppy, it still gives them some comfort and confidence in their new environment.

―――――

ONCE YOU NOTICE that the puppy is sleeping pretty good and you would like to get them to start sleeping on their own, it is important to do so in small steps. For example, if the puppy is sleeping in your bed and you want to get them to start sleeping in their crate in another room, the first step would be to get the puppy used to being in the crate during the day. Then you can move the crate to the side of the bed and have them stay there at night.

―――――

AFTER THE PUPPY has been able to do that, then you can move the puppy and the crate to their permanent sleeping room on a night when they are really tired. This is a day that you should really get them extra tired so that they do not nap during the day. This makes it more likely that the puppy will just go straight into the crate and fall asleep without any issues because they are too tired to fight.

WITH A SMALL PUPPY, you will need to get up and take them to the potty at least once or twice a night. When you do this, it is best to get them while they are still asleep or when they are reasonably calm if you can. This makes it much easier to get the puppy to fall asleep when they are done. If you wait too long and the puppy is screaming and freaking out, you will find that they are now too wound up to go to sleep and it could lead to a very long night for you.

FROM HERE, it is time to decide which method you would like to choose so that you can get your puppy to sleep well through the night. All puppies and their owners will be different, so you may find that you like one method better than the other, or you may need to do some trial and error. No one method is better than the other so go ahead and try them out and see what works the best for you!

6

THE BEST SLEEP TRAINING
TECHNIQUES FOR YOUR PUPPY

As we mentioned before, there are actually three best methods that you can use to help get your puppy to fall asleep and stay asleep at night. None of the methods are better than any other, you just need to decide which one you like the best. The three methods that you can choose from include the following;

The Alarm Clock Method

THIS IS CONSIDERED one of the best methods to use because it is so simple and you will not have to remember a ton of steps to get it done. It is easy, but maybe not fun, but it is considered really effective and simple to follow with.

WHEN YOU USE THIS METHOD, you will be able to take control over the overnight schedule for your puppy by setting the alarm clock to help wake you up each night. It does not matter if the puppy wakes up or not. The point here is to beat the puppy to the goal. If your puppy wakes up before you, then it is because they are uncomfortable and they will probably get hyper and freak out, which will make it really hard for you to get them back to sleep in the end.

IF YOU SET an alarm and wake up before the puppy does to take them out, you are able to save a lot of hassle. First, the puppy will still be sleepy and easier to get to bed in the middle of the night when they are done. Second, the puppy never gets in the habit of crying and barking in order to wake you up.

WHEN YOU FIRST BRING THE puppy home, it is likely that you will need to have the alarm go off for you a few times each night. For a puppy who is between seven to nine weeks old, you will need to do this ever two hours. Once the puppy is between nine weeks to fourteen weeks, you can do it every three hours. And puppies that are over fourteen weeks will go about every four hours.

OF COURSE, these are pretty general guidelines for a brand-new puppy. Some need to go more often and some need to go less. Take the time to learn the schedule of your puppy so you can set the alarm at the right time and take them out before they wake up and get too hyper. If you have already had the puppy for a few weeks, then it is likely that you already know how long the puppy is able to hold it, so base the schedule you use on that.

———

So, if the puppy has gotten into the habit of waking you up with barks and crying every four hours, then you should set the alarm for every three or three and a half hours. The exact time is not important, as long as you make it your goal to catch the puppy when they are likely to need to go, but before they get to a critical point of howling and barking.

———

Once the puppy is on a good schedule of waking up at intervals throughout the night, you are going to work on pushing it to get the puppy to sleep longer. In the beginning, you may be tired for waking up so often, but this is the part of the program when the work will pay off. Since you are the one who is in control of the schedule at night, you are able to adjust the wake-up times and then work through until you get the puppy to start sleeping through the whole night.

———

FOR MOST PUPPIES, once you are able to wake up the puppy and get them to go potty at night on a schedule, without accidents, howling, or barking, for three nights, then it is time to move on. However, for puppies who are very young when you go with this process, it is better to wait for about five nights in a row before moving on.

WHEN YOU ARE ready to extend this, you will want to extend how long you wait before waking them up by about thirty minutes each time. So, if you were successful at waking the puppy up at 1:00, 3:00, and 5:00, you will now go through and wake them up at 1:30, 4, and 6:30. Once you have another three to five nights of this, you can increase it all by another thirty minutes again.

YOU WILL KEEP MOVING these potty trips ahead until the last trip that you have starts to coincide with the time that you want to get up in the morning. At this point, you should not be down to two potty trips instead of having to do three. And over time, you will go down to one until you are finally down to none.

ONE DOWNSIDE that you should know about this method is that you may get up more often at night and take the puppy to the bathroom more times than they really need. This is especially true if you start this from the moment you bring the puppy home and you have no idea what their schedule is about. In the long-term, there is nothing wrong with the puppy being let out more often than they need to go. On the short-term, you will miss out on more sleep, but this process does not last long and you will make it up.

The Light Sleeper Method

IF YOU DO NOT like the idea of setting your alarm clock to wake up all those times in the middle of the night, then it may be time to try a different method. Some people don't like the other method because they see that waking up by an alarm many times at night is stressful or that they are wasting their time by taking the puppy outside too often. The following method is going to work great if you are a pretty light sleeper and you are going to let the puppy sleep near you.

WHEN IT COMES to the light sleeper method, you are going to let the puppy tell you when they are ready to go potty so that you are able to take them to the right potty spots when needed. When you start to hear the puppy moving around in their pen or their crate at night, or if you hear a bit of light panting or whimpering, then you must get out of bed as soon as possible and take the puppy out.

TO SEE success with this method, you need to be a really light sleeper so that you can notice when the puppy starts to move around. If you sleep too deeply, then the puppy will start to wail and shriek to be taken out, and then they will be stressed and wide awake when they are done. In addition, this will teach the puppy that it is fine to wake you up with hysterics, and this will get old pretty fast when the puppy decides they want attention later on.

THE NICE PART about using this method is that if you use it the right way, you an save some hassle and will only take the puppy out when they really need to go. If you get one of those puppies who can go for longer periods for their age without needing to be let out, this method will allow you to get more sleep because you will not need to make unnecessary trips outside, resulting in a puppy that sleeps through the night very quickly.

HOWEVER, there are a few downsides to using this method. If the puppy does not move around a lot when they wake up, or if you find that you are not really as light of a sleeper as you though, you could end up with a puppy who will work themselves up to crying before you even notice something is wrong.

IF THIS HAPPENS, it is still a good idea to wake up and take the puppy out, but it may be time to rethink whether this is a good method if this happens more than once or twice. Another issue is that you may have a puppy who doesn't want to wake you or make a lot of noise, and who will instead just have an accident right where they are without you noticing. If this does happen to you, then this isn't the right method for your little puppy and it may be best to work with the alarm clock method to help get on a schedule.

The Heavy Sleeper Method

THE THIRD METHOD that you can choose is the heavy sleeper method. This is usually not seen as the most effective method to sleep train your puppy, but it can work for some people. This is sometimes the only method that will work if you have a puppy that is really fussy, loud, or resistant to other approaches. This is often a method that you will resort to when the others do not work.

FOR THIS METHOD, spend the first three to five nights sleeping with the puppy so that they can get used to being in your home and their new surroundings. When that is done, this method will require that the puppy will sleep in another room. Pick out a room that is at least far enough away from you that you will not be able to hear them crying. You can place the puppy into a pen, a crate, or a small puppy proofed room, such as a laundry room, depending on what housebreaking program you choose.

No matter what room you choose to go with, it is important that you make sure that the puppy is getting a comfortable place to stick with. You should also make sure that the puppy is also getting enough chances to go to the potty during the night. However, if you hear the puppy scream bloody murder because they are not that fond of sleeping at night, you will just leave them in the other room so that they are able to cry it out.

This method requires the puppy to be in another room so that you can ignore the crying and get some sleep. Allow them to go to the bathroom if they need it, but some puppies just like to be loud and fight going to sleep. This could easily keep you up at night and can make it difficult on everyone. If you are not a heavy sleeper, you can turn on a sound machine, a loud fan, a radio, or even wear some ear plugs. If you do this, set an alarm clock that is loud enough that you can hear it, and then use the alarm clock method so that the puppy can go out to the potty at the right times.

AFTER YOU TAKE the puppy out for their bathroom break based on the alarm clock method, put the puppy right back to the crate or pen or room, and then go back to bed. You will be surprised at how quickly the puppy will get over this screaming phase, especially when they realize that their noise is not really accomplishing it. Keep in mind that some puppies will get over this in a few days and others may take a few weeks.

THE GOOD NEWS that the puppy will get over this, even if it seems like it takes some time. It will just take each puppy a different amount of time. Once the puppy has resigned themselves to the fate and starts to sleep at night, you get the choice to have them stay sleeping int hat same area, or you can move them closer to you or to a new location if you choose. You just need to be able to get through the whining part and separating out the puppy from you can make that process a bit easier.

THERE ARE some downsides to this. The big downside to this is that if the puppy does end up waking up at night and makes noise because they really need to go potty, even if it is not on your schedule, it is likely that you are not going to be able to hear them. This means that you are going to run into a big risk of the puppy having an accident because they are not able to go out when they really need to go.

You could also run into some issues with your neighbors that may not be happy with the wailing that the puppy has. You may be surprised at how far that noise is going to travel. If you are not careful with this, you could end up with a neighbor who is upset and banging on your door in the middle of the night. Before you go with this method, consider who else may be bothered by the crying puppy if you put them in another room and ignore them. If the puppy only whines for a few nights, you are probably fine. But if they are really resistant and cry for a few weeks, the neighbors are not likely to be that happy.

These three methods are meant to help you get your puppy to start sleeping through the night. Each of them will take some time to accomplish and will not get the puppy to start sleeping through the night in one night. But with some work and some dedication, and by following the suggestions in each of the steps, you will be able to get that puppy to sleep through the night in less time than you would imagine.

7

WHAT TO DO IF IT'S NOT WORKING?

I f you have turned straight to this page because you are already in the middle of the mess with a puppy who won't sleep, you may be in panic mode. You will not be able to go through and try any of the tips until you can read this book, and that will not happen until tomorrow. So, you may be wondering what steps you can take to help make things easier today.

THE FIRST STEP that you should take is to go pick up the puppy and give them a little bit of attention. Depending on how much time you have spent with them so far today and how active they have been, you may also need to go and get them a bit of exercise. Now, you may be thinking that this is a bad thing and you may be teaching the puppy that they will get their way if they make a lot of noise. However, at this point, you need to do it anyway.

FOR TONIGHT, until you are able to get some time to read the book and implement the steps that we talked about above, you are going to just give in so that you and the puppy can get a little bit of relief for the night. When you wake up in the morning, it is time to start it all fresh and use the tips that are in this guidebook. Since you have not even started on the training program at all, getting the puppy this once when they are crying is not really going to undermine anything. Plenty of people do this for weeks before they start on a training program so doing it once is not that big of a deal. Once you pick one of the above sleep training programs, do not do this anymore. But for tonight, so that the two of you can get some sleep, it is just fine to give the puppy some love and attention.

Now, if your puppy did not get a lot of napping in during the day and they were pretty active, at this point they are probably tired but have just become too stressed out and scared about the new sleeping environment. You may find that the puppy will easily settle down once you let them spend some time near you. You can choose whether you would like to sleep on the floor next to the pen or crate to get them used to this new area. You can also tether them in the bed so they don't move and fall off. Sometimes moving the crate by the bed or elevating it on a chair so that the puppy can see you will help. Pick the method that works the best for you when it comes to puppy.

If you do this and you are a bit worried about how the puppy may wake up everyone in the family if you place them in your room, or you do not like the idea of letting a dog be in your room, you can just set up camp in the living room. For this, you would simply get comfortable on the floor or on the couch, and let the puppy sleep next to you. You can also let the puppy be in the crate and you can try sticking your fingers in to let the puppy know you are there.

THE POINT here is that many times the puppy will calm down when they know that someone is there and that they are not all alone in a new environment. You may have to be uncomfortable for a night or sleep somewhere new in the home, but it is often enough to get the puppy to fall asleep and then everyone in the home can get some peace.

ON THE OTHER HAND, if your puppy is still awake late at night and they did get plenty of naps in during the day, they may not want to settle down even after spending some time near you. This is most likely because the puppy has plenty of energy to use and they want to go and burn it off. The best thing to do, even if you are overly exhausted at this point, is to help them get that energy to go away. You can have some playtime or take them on a walk so that you do not have the puppy barking and waking up everyone.

No one wants to go on a walk or play with a puppy when it is time to go to bed, but this is the best option if you have a puppy who slept too much during the day and has a lot of leftover energy to get rid of. If you do not take the time to wear out the puppy, then they are just going to wake everyone else up and mess around all night. It may be three in the morning, but as soon as you get onto some of the steps that we talked about earlier, then you will no longer have to have this active time so early. Once you have been able to get the puppy back to sleep and settled down, then you can start to follow the instructions for puppy sleep training to get through the rest of the night.

Now, if your puppy went through a day that was busy and they did not have a lot of naps, and they are already sleeping right by you, but you still notice that they are freaking out, it may be time to change up the arrangements that you picked for sleeping. If the puppy is in a carte or a pen, they may not be comfortable in that yet and need to be tethered to a bed. Or, if you have already let them sleep by you for a few nights to help them adjust, you may want to consider trying the heavy sleeper training method so that they learn how to get used to their environment without disturbing your sleep.

———

ONE NOTE, if the puppy is brand new to your home or they are showing signs that they are extremely stressed, then do not use the heavy sleeper method. If you notice shaking, trying to escape from a pen or crate in a manner that will hurt them, or lots of drooling, then you do not want to use that method. Instead, let the puppy stick next to you so that they do not get stressed out and then consider using a dog trainer in the next few days. You will find that severe anxiety issues like this are hard to solve all on your own without experience so if your puppy is showing these signs, it may be time to bring in the professionals.

———

IN ADDITION, if your puppy has been sleeping well and then they wake up all of a sudden with cries, this is considered normal. You should just need to take them out to go to the bathroom and put them right back to bed. You only need to go with the instructions that we 'talked about above if your puppy has already gone to the bathroom and is still freaking out, or if you just can't calm them down. You can always give them comfort for now and do whatever it takes to get some sleep, and then skip on to reading the tips in this book and following them later.

———

AND REMEMBER, while you are doing all of this, make sure that the puppy is not crying because they are hurt or sick. Sometimes the crying is because they are scared or trying to get your attention, and this is normal. But if you see signs that your puppy is not feeling good or is in pain and they seem to be crying because of this, then it is important to get them to a vet.

———

WHEN IT COMES to getting your puppy to sleep, you need to pick out one of the methods that we talked about above and then stick with it. Some puppies will learn within a few nights and others will take a little bit longer, but all of these methods will work. But if you just got this book and you have not had time to read anything except this chapter, it is fine to give the puppy some attention and company. You can always start on your chosen method tomorrow, but just try to get some good sleep for you and for the puppy for tonight.

The desperate measures

Now, if you have gone through all of the methods that are in this book and you are not getting good results after some reasonable time, you may be at a loss for what you should do next. It is rare for this to happen, but with some puppies it does. If this is the case, it may be time to take it to the next level.

At this point, you may want to consider working with a professional dog trainer to help you out. Some will be willing to take the puppy home and do some of the initial steps that are needed for sleep training. This is only recommended if the trainer is going to have the puppy stay at their home, rather than in a boarding kennel. You should also check with the trainer to make sure that they have experience with doing this and that they have a training philosophy that matches up with your own. If you are interested in doing this,

Talk to your vet or a friend to get some recommendations.

IF YOU ARE lucky enough to find someone who works for this, you could even have them do the first few nights of sleep training, or you can try a friend or family member to help. It is possible that you know someone who is able and willing to do the work and can make it a bit easier for you. Either way, it can take some of the pressure from you and make sleep training your puppy so much easier on the whole family.

NOW, you may be worried about sending your puppy off for a few nights for training. This can be hard to send away the puppy and you may feel that you are giving up the responsibility that you should handle. However, in the real world, you sometimes need help and can't do it all on your own. Instead of having a few bad days and nights and then returning the puppy, getting some help at the beginning can make it easier and can make you and the puppy so much happier.

THE GOOD NEWS IS, that it is rare to find an adult dog that doesn't know how to sleep through the night. So, even if you have kind of a rocky start with the puppy and sleep training takes longer than you think it should, the good news is that your puppy will eventually learn how to sleep through the night!

AFTERWORD

Bringing home a new puppy is such a big deal in most families. It allows you and your family to bond with a new addition and can be a great role of responsibility for everyone involved. However, brining home that puppy can come with a few hard days and nights as you try to help the puppy get used to their new surroundings and get some sleep at night.

If you have a new puppy and you either want to start off right with some good sleep training techniques, or you are tired of being up most of the night dealing with the puppy, then this guidebook is the one for you. It took some time to discuss the different methods that you can use to sleep train your puppy and made it easier than ever to finally get your puppy to sleep through the night. There are three main strategies that you can use that will be golden and help you and your puppy to adjust to sleeping through the night.

When you are ready to help your puppy learn how to sleep properly through the night at any age, make sure to pick up this guidebook to help you get started.

Made in the USA
Middletown, DE
12 January 2021